CHINESE CARPETS AND RUGS.

WOOL CARPET

shows in the field the eight buddhist symbols of happy augury. The medalion in the centre represents two phoenix in the Yin-Yang form, enclosed by clouds. The corner ornaments, composed of the "fragrant finger of Buddha," the sceptre and the vase, mean "happiness, long life and peace according to desire".
The border is composed of dragon's heads placed between seawaves and mountains.

CHINESE
CARPETS AND RUGS

by ADOLF HACKMACK

translation by L. ARNOLD

CHARLES E. TUTTLE COMPANY
Rutland, Vermont & Tokyo, Japan

Representatives

Continental Europe: BOXERBOOKS, INC., *Zurich*

British Isles: PRENTICE-HALL INTERNATIONAL, INC., *London*

Australasia: BOOK WISE (AUSTRALIA) PTY. LTD.
104-108 Sussex Street, Sydney 2000

Published by the Charles E. Tuttle Company, Inc.
of Rutland, Vermont & Tokyo, Japan
with editorial offices at
Suido 1-chome, 2-6, Bunkyo-ku, Tokyo, Japan

© *1980 by Charles E. Tuttle Co., Inc.*

Library of Congress Catalog Card No. 77-83943

International Standard Book No. 0-8048-1258-6

First edition, 1924 by
La Librairie Française, Tientsin
First Tuttle edition, 1980

PRINTED IN JAPAN

TO H. C. AUGUSTESEN.

CONTENTS

LIST OF ILLUSTRATIONS

LIST OF ILLUSTRATIONS (CONTINUED)

PUBLISHER'S FOREWORD
TO THE NEW EDITION

It is always a pleasure to rescue a worthwhile book from an oblivion that it by no means deserves and, by doing so, to bring satisfaction to readers who have long sought for it with no hope of success. Adolf Hackmack's *Chinese Carpets and Rugs* is an example of that kind of book, and it is presented here, in a faithful reprint edition, with considerable pride.

The fascination of Chinese carpets and rugs needs no introduction to a Western audience, for both laymen and experienced collectors have long since found enchantment in one of China's most elegant products. Even as early as more than half a century ago, these superb examples of the Chinese weaver's art were being exported to almost every quarter of the globe. From the beginning, they were greatly admired for the splendid colors of their traditional designs. Most admirers of Chinese carpets and rugs are aware that the conventions of pattern employed in them have inner and peculiar meanings of their own, but it is not always easy, without a certain degree of study and experience, to understand the significance of these patterns. It was for the purpose of explaining such patterns that Mr. Hackmack wrote his book.

First published in the famous rug-making city of Tientsin more than fifty years ago in a limited edition, the book has unjustly been out of print for far too long. It has been the object of eager and futile search by many collectors, and its reappearance here is certain to be welcomed by all discerning students of carpet weaving in one of its most famous and delightful forms. The publisher is grateful for the opportunity to bring it to light once again.

PREFACE.

In recent years Chinese carpets have been exported to nearly every quarter of the globe. These carpets have been greatly admired on account of the colours of their traditional designs, but the significance attached to them has not always been understood by the public Most people are acquainted with the Persian carpet and know that its very conventionalised patterns have an inner and peculiar meaning of their own. The same may be said of the patterns seen on Chinese carpets, and it is to explain their meanings that this little volume was put together.

Tientsin, June 1923

ADOLF HACKMACK

TEMPLE OF HEAVEN, PEKING.

CHAPTER I
THE DEVELOPMENT OF CARPET WEAVING.

CHAPTER I
THE DEVELOPMENT OF CARPET WEAVING.

*C*ARPET weaving has been carried on from the earliest times in the Western and Northern parts of China, Chinese Turkestan, Tibet and the Province of Kansu. The art of carpet weaving came probably from Central Asia to Chinese Turkestan, the native home of the Turks, and from there, by way of Tibet, was introduced into Kansu. The inhabitants of those regions, composed mostly of nomad tribes, used carpets in their tentlike dwellings in a twofold capacity — as protection against the inclement weather and as decoration, thereby combining use with ornamentation.

The materials employed for the weaving varied according to the purpose for which the carpet was intended, being either of sheep's wool, goat or camel's hair or yak hair. Beautiful so-called prayer-rugs were made in Tibet, being ornamented with suitable designs, such as are seen spread in Buddhist temples and in the Mosques of the Mohammedans where the Faithful kneel when making their devotions. Among specimens of the loveliest carpets should be reckoned the saddle-covers made in the town of Ning hsia fu on the Huangho. They are greatly prized alike by Mongol chieftains and by Chinese mandarins. The saddle-covers are most artistic both through the treatment of their materials and through the grouping of their colours.

As the Carpet-weavers' skill in their work increased, more costly materials came to be used in the manufacture and thus, besides sheep's wool, silk thread was introduced.

CHINESE CARPETS AND RUGS

Old Chinese silk carpets can be distinguished from the Indian, Persian and Turkish only by their designs. Old Chinese wool carpets resemble in quality and make those of India, and like the latter, have a cotton warp of about 80 to 120 threads to one foot but are of thicker pile than Persian carpets, and differ again from the Turkish which have a wool warp instead of cotton.

A great impetus was given to the art of carpet weaving in the period of the last dynasty. The celebrated Emperor Kang Hsi (1662-1722), whose aim was to foster every branch of industry in the land, invited painters to Peking, whom he commissioned to improve and enrich designs for the porcelain, weaving and carpet industries.

What was begun by this ruler was continued by his grandson, Ch'ien Lung (1736-1796) who, being a lover of the luxurious and beautiful, appreciated carpets at their true worth and gave great orders for them to the home industry, besides purchasing lovely pieces from abroad. In addition to this, carpets were also presented to the emperor by the neighbouring Mongolian tribes by way of tribute. Most of the carpets in the Peking palaces date from his reign, and even to day are magnificent examples. The carpet weaving of Kansu is also said to have been introduced at this period into Peking, the northern coastal towns and the Province of Shantung.

In every Chinese province to which the art spread, and the adjacent countries which with them comprise the Carpet Weaving District (see map), the industry took a firm hold and flourishes to the present day.

THE DEVELOPMENT OF CARPET WEAVING.

Chinese Turkestan, the original home of the art, rich in wool and silk, still retains by its wonderful Products a pre-eminent position in the industry. Besides the manufacture of what is required for use in the country itself, a great number of carpets are expressly made for export to foreign lands. The weaving in Chinese Turkestan is a home industry in which every member of the family, male and female, has a share. The most important carpet markets of Turkestan are Yarkand, Khotan, Kashgar and Turfan.

Tibet is not so important as Turkestan in the carpet industry. It is mostly carried on in the capital, Lhassa, and the article chiefly made has been for generations the prayer-rugs which are sold to the numerous pilgrims who travel to that town.

In the Province of Kansu carpet weaving is also a home industry and is carried on more generally than in Tibet. The most popular manufactures are warm wool carpets for daily use, for which sheep's wool and camel's hair are imported from Mongolia. The chief trade centres are Ning hsia fu and Suchou.

Of the north-eastern provinces, Chihli and Shantung are the most important in the industry. Here carpets are not a home product, as in other parts of the "Carpet District", but are manufactured as a regular article of commerce in factories, where men only are employed. The chief centres of the trade in Chihli are Tientsin, Peking and Kalgan.

In Shantung the art of carpet weaving found ideal conditions in which to thrive, owing to the wealth of the region in material, both silk and wool. This province is one of the greatest wool-producing districts, its total yearly produce being over 1.500.000 lbs. Its sheep, bred principally in the mountainous regions of the West and East, number about half a million head. The silk thread of Shantung which is used in silk rugs is celebrated the world over as "Pongee" or "Shantung Silk". Sericulture in various forms is carried on all over the province and energetically fostered by the Government, which promotes the cultivation of mulberry trees, on the leaves of which the silkworm is fed.

With such exceptionally great wealth of wool and silk materials to hand it was only natural that the Provincial Government of Shantung should show in a practical form its interest in the industry. About 1900 the Industrial School (Kung-I-Chü) for carpet weavers in Tsinanfu was established and a suitable place set apart for actual carpet weaving. A teacher from Kansu was engaged to instruct the youth of Shantung in the art. It should be observed that carpets turned out by this establishment have about 90 threads to the foot and are noted for their careful finish.

Owing to the increasing export trade, the production of carpets has increased continously in volume during recent years, especially during the years of the Great War, when American carpet traders, hitherto accustomed to drawing their supplies from Persia, turned their attention to China. Tientsin has now become the chief export centre for the Chinese carpet. Some 500 great and small factories now make carpets there. In 1913 the value of the Export trade was Taels 90.000 as against

Taels	420.270	in 1919
„	1.133.000	in 1920
„	1.658.650	in 1921
„	2.532.000	in 1922
„	3.795.000	in 1923.

THE DEVELOPMENT OF CARPET WEAVING

The bulk of the export goes to North America, but it can only be a question of time until Europe also will be interested in these carpets which are not only the product of an artistic handicraft but seem to possess an endless life for wear and tear.

Lü Tung-pin,

Taoist genius with his sword of supernatural power.

(See text, page 19)

CHAPTER II
CARPET DESIGNS

CHAPTER 2
CARPET DESIGNS.

*W*E may take Central Asia as the original district of manufacture. Carpet designs, however, owe their origin to the districts to which the art of carpet weaving spread. In the West we have the Persian and Turkish; in the South the Indian and in the East the Chinese.

The designs of Chinese carpets are all older than carpet making itself in China, for they are derived from those used in silk weaving. These in their turn have the same origin as the paintings found on old Chinese pottery. Many designs seen on porcelains are therefore to be found in carpets.

Silk designs can be traced back until lost in antiquity. Indeed, as far back as in the records of China's trade with the Romans, mention is made of silk fabrics of "splendid designs". In the SHU-CHING, the classical Book of History, are to be found descriptions of ornamentations on banners and on the silken garments of officials. In the time of the Sung Dynasty (A. D. 960 to 1279) the names of more than 50 designs are given, of which many are still used in carpets, among them being: "The Dragon in Water", "Dragon entwined between Flowers", "Dragon and Phoenix", "Dragon in Medallions", "Tortoise-shell Background", "Lotus Flowers", "Floral Symbol of Long Life", "Musical Instruments", "Lion with Ball", "Aquatic Plants and Playing Fishes" and "Tree Peonies". Combinations of written characters signifying happiness and groups of symbols signifying good luck are also given.

It is not only through illustrations in old writings that we can trace the age and origin of these designs. Evidence is also afforded us by the many old monuments of China, which are richly adorned with carvings in similar designs. The fresco paintings and remnants of fabrics brought to light at Turfan by the excavations carried on by Grünwedel, furnish us with a vivid picture of the designs generally in vogue at that golden period of the textile art in Turkestan. Most of the carpet designs of to-day are to be seen in these ornaments of some thousand years ago. In his report on archaeological work done at Idikutshari in Chinese Turkestan in the winter of 1902/3, Gruenwedel says : "I cannot help suggesting what a wealth of material would appear were one able to devote the necessary time to arranging systematically all the temple ornamentations that still survive in the carpet weaving of to-day". As a complement of the pieces of fabric excavated at Turfan we would point to the remnants of carpet fabrics, dating from the 8th century, which are housed in the Shosoin Imperial Treasury at Nara, in Japan, which will be described later in these pages.

Thanks to the tenacity with which the Chinese cling to all that is ancient we still find these old designs on the weaving looms, lending to the Chinese carpet a very special charm, not only on account of its great antiquity of design, but also on account of its peculiarity and unique characteristics, retained through centuries and making of each carpet a surviving evidence of an historical past.

Chinese carpet designs are in part closely related to the legends and the various religions of the people, and in part taken from their trees and flowers.

For a description of these the following divisions will perhaps be found most useful :—

A) Geometrical designs
B) Designs derived from ancient Chinese tradition

C) Designs derived from Taoism
D) Designs derived from Buddhism
E) Miscellaneous symbols
F) Tree and flower patterns.

A) GEOMETRICAL DESIGNS.

The geometrical designs are among the oldest of patterns and are mostly of pre-historic origin. They are chiefly used as border ornamentations and are to be found on most carpets.

The Pearl border ([1] *chu-pien*) Fig. 1 is used as a frame to the field of the carpet, separating it from the border ornamentation, as shown in Fig. 52 and 54.

The Chinese Line ([2] *han-wên*) Fig. 2a and 2b also known as the Chinese T-pattern (2a) or Key design (2b), is used in both the forms shown. It is, like the Pearl border, used to finish off the field of the carpet. According to Fr. Birth such designs were used on the stone urns of the Chou Dynasty (B. C. 1122 to 255). The Chinese Line, as shown in Figures 47, 48, 50b, 51 and 54, gives only a few examples of the manifold forms in use.

The Recurring Line ([3] *hui-wên*) is similar to the Chinese line and like it used as a border ornamentation. Its corresponding geometrical corner and centre ornaments are also applied in very diverse forms, of which some are given in Fig. 3a to 3c.

The Dice Pattern ([4] *shai-tzu-kuai*) Fig. 4 is employed as a field design.

---

[1] 珠邊　　[2] 漢紋　　[3] 回紋　　[4] 賽子塊

13

The Circle Pattern Fig. 5 is also called the "Golden Coin design" (⁵*chin ch'ien*), because the circle with the square in the centre resembles the old Chinese pierced coins. (compare with Fig. 21b).

The Swastika (⁶*wan-tzu*) signifies luck. In combination with other symbols it means "ten-thousandfold". It is represented either singly (Fig. 6 a), in a square (Fig. 6 b), or in a circle or again continuously in border ornamentation or as a ground design. It is not too much to say that of all the symbols mentioned this is the one most often met with in carpets, and fancy has run riot in its grouping and composition for design. In the form linked together as a continuous pattern it is called by the Chinese ⁷*wan-tzu-pu-tao-t'ou,* i. e. "endless luck". As a border pattern it is used as in Fig. 47, 48, 49, 50 b, 50 c and 52 ; as a field design, as in Fig. 50 a.

B) DESIGNS DERIVED FROM ANCIENT CHINESE TRADITION.

The Ancient Tradition is also called the Cult of Confucius, not because it originated with him, but because he collected and collated precepts which were partly in existence long before his time, and which through his name came to be invested with a new value.

Confucius, a contemporary of Pythagoras, was born in the year B. C. 551 at Chü-fu in the State of Lu, part of the present day Province of Shantung. The influence which he exercised and still exercises on the Chinese people is incalculable. According to ancient tradition the highest veneration was that due to Heaven, Earth and

⁵ 金錢　⁶ 萬字　⁷ 萬字不到頭

the Forces of Nature. Even to this day, the Head of the State sacrifices once a year to these divinities in the Temple of Heaven (see Illustration).

The Dragon (⁸ *lung*) Fig. 7. This celebrated symbol of China ranks first among all the ornamentations on carpets in the Peking palaces, as also in fabrics, embroideries, bronzes, porcelains and public buildings.

There are different kinds of dragons: the five-clawed, formerly reserved for the Imperial court ; the four-clawed ; the winged, and the horned and the hornless dragons of heaven, rivers and mountains, each of which is represented in its proper element, between clouds, waves or hills. As sovereign of the forces of nature it is much dreaded. It is regarded as divine and is particularly venerated in regions which are frequently subject to inundations.

On carpets the dragon is depicted in various forms according to its position in the centre, the corners or the border of the piece. The central field of the carpet in Fig. 49 is decorated with a remarkable dragon design which is said to have been evolved in the Sung Dynasty (960 to 1279) at which period decorative art reached its height. The dragon is represented either singly, in pairs, or with a phoenix (Fig. 18) for contrast. The combination of these two creatures is a favourite motif and means "dragon and phoenix heralding happiness". The ball usually shown before the dragon symbolises thunder and lightning, as author of which it is regarded (see Fig. 52).

---

⁸

The Thunder Line (⁹ *lei-wen*) Fig. 8a to 8e. For thunder there was the pre-historic hieroglyphic design shaped something like a spiral (Fig. 8a). It later, as in the Chinese written character, acquired an angular form (Fig. 8b), which was united in pairs (Fig. 8c and 8d) for decorative purposes. By uniting the latter signs (8c and 8d) for border ornamentation the Chinese meander is obtained (Fig. 8e). In this connection it should however be observed that it differs from the Greek meander pattern in that its composition is a broken and not a continuous one.

For thunder there is, besides this symbol, the ball shewn before the dragon in Fig. 7, which is called the "pearl of the dragon" (¹⁰ *lung-chu*.) In this design the symbol for thunder (Fig. 8a) is composed of a revolving wheel, signifying the rolling movement of thunder, while by the addition of certain flourishes the idea of lightning is also indicated. Another explanation is that the original figure for thunder is a clapper on a metal disk, which causes the clash of thunder.

The Cloud Design (¹¹ *yün-wên*) Fig. 9a to 9i. This peculiar pattern, which is rarely seen outside of Asiatic countries, has been from early times a favourite motif in Chinese carpets, especially where vacant spaces have to be filled in. The design can be applied in any size and number. The illustrations under No. 9 show a few of the many possible conventionalised forms of this design as central and corner ornaments. It is usually employed in combination with the heavenly dragon or the phoenix; often as a frame to them in narrow

⁹ 雷紋　¹⁰ 龍珠　¹¹ 雲紋

16

border ornamentations (see Fig. 52), in which case it is called (*[12]yün tou-erh*), the cloud-border, and given in innumberable forms, (see Fig. 42).

The Water Design, (*[13]shui-wên*). Still water is represented by half-circles, one superimposed on the other (Fig. 11); while sea waves are depicted by angular figures similarly placed (Fig. 12). The form of the waves is indicated by small clouds over the angular figures. The water pattern is mostly combined with representations of dragons rising from its midst; but it is also much used in varied forms by itself as a border design (see Fig. 48).

Fire and Lightning, Fig. 13a to 13c are depicted by scrolls in the shape of blazing flames, which are used both as centre and as border designs.

Mountains and Crags, Fig. 14a to 14c are shown either rising from the water, or in combination with the mountain dragon. While temples are erected in the towns to the gods of these forces of nature, the mountain spirits are worshipped upon the five highest mountains of China.

The Male and Female Elements of Being (*[14]Yin and Yang*). This is the double figure in the centre of Fig. 15. The *Yin* is the dark, female reproductive element and the *Yang* the light, male procreative element. The theory of these cosmic dual forces is extremely old; and it is to their interaction that the Chinese ascribe the existence of the entire universe.

---

[12] 雲頭兒　　[13] 水紋　　[14] 陰陽

The Eight Trigrams of Divination. ([15] *pa-kua*) Fig. 15. Representations of the *Yin-yang* are usually surrounded with these eight characters. They are composed of whole and broken lines, and belong to the oldest forms of the Chinese written language. The classical Book of Changes (*I-Ching*) is written in these characters, which have played a great part in the demonology of China, while at the same time they serve the purpose of fortune telling divination. The three unbroken lines ≡≡≡≡≡≡ mean heaven, after which, reading from the right, the rest mean clouds, thunder, mountains, water, fire, earth and wind.

The Sceptre ([16] *ju-i*) of the supreme deity of Heaven Fig. 10. This symbol of his power is a favourite ornament. The head of the sceptre represents a cloud. As a symbol it signifies "May all wishes and hopes be fulfilled".

C) DESIGNS DERIVED FROM TAOISM

Taoism, founded by the philosopher Lao-Tzu (born B. C. 604) is the teaching of *Tao* — the Way — the origin and the ultimate aim of being. In later times pure Taoism became corrupted by an admixture of superstition in the form of alchemy and the search for the elixir of life. The principal aim of its teaching is the prolongation of life. The symbols derived from this cult nearly all, therefore, concern the subject of longevity.

The Attributes of the "Eight Genii" ([17] *pa-pao*) Fig. 17 a to 17 h. The "Eight Genii" or immortal guardian spirits ([18] *pa-hsien*) are

---

[15] 八卦   [16] 如意   [17] 八寶   [18] 八仙

CARPET DESIGNS.

disciples of Lao-Tzu. They are usually shown amidst beautiful scenery representing paradise, and are favourite subjects of painting and silk embroidery. In carpets the representation of their attributes alone seems to be considered sufficient.

They are as follows:

a) The fan with which [19] *Chung Li-chüan* revives the souls of the dead (see page 32, with peach)

b) The sword of supernatural power carried by [20] *Lü Tung-pin* (see page 8)

c) The magic pilgrim's staff and gourd of [21] *Li Tieh-kuai*

d) The bamboo castanets of [22] *Ts'ao Kuo-chiu*

e) The flower basket carried by [23] *Lan Ts'ai-ho*

f) The bamboo tube and rods of [24] *Chang Kuo* (see page 38)

g) The flute of [25] *Han Hsiang-tzu*

h) The lotus-flower of [26] *Ho Hsien-ku* (see page 43)

The eight immortal genii, like their attributes, have a long history, the narration of which would lead us too far afield here.

The Phoenix ([27] *fêng-huang*) Fig. 18. This fabulous creature signifies benevolence and goodness. As messenger of the eight genii it is the medium of intercourse between them and the living. Its appearance heralds good times and happy events. It is a sort of heron

[19] 鍾離權 [20] 呂洞賓 [21] 李鐵拐 [22] 曹國舅
[23] 藍采和 [24] 張果 [25] 韓湘子
[26] 何仙姑 [27] 鳳凰

with the shimmering feathers of the golden pheasant and the tail of a peacock, and it is regarded as the king of birds. It is frequently placed as a contrast to the dragon and represented with a peony in its beak; or else as a pair, in the form of the *Yin-Yang,* as a central ornament (see Fig. 52).

The *Stag* ([28] *lu*) is the symbol of longevity and prosperity. It is often represented as bearing in its mouth the sacred magic fungus ([29] *ling-chih-ts'ao*) through the eating of which it attains long life (see Fig. 47).

The *Crane* ([30] *hsien hao*) is one of the commonest symbols of longevity. Fable credits it with a life of thousands of years. After 600 years it requires only liquid nourishment, and after 2000 years is said to assume a black colour. It is usually depicted with the Stag. (Compare Fig. 47.)

The *Peach* ([31] *t'ao*) is the fruit of life, also the food of the eight immortal genii. It symbolises longevity and is often represented together with other symbols.

D) DESIGNS DERIVED FROM BUDDHISM.

In its more general sense Buddhism was introduced from India into China in the first centuries of the Christian era. Its teaching exercised a great influence, not only on religious thought but on art and architecture.

---

[28] 鹿   [29] 靈芝草   [30] 仙鶴   [31] 桃

The Lion (³²*shih-tzu*) Fig. 19, is a fabulous animal of threatening aspect figuring as the defender of the law and protector of Buddhist sacred buildings. When represented with a ball in its paw, this creature is regarded as the male, and when holding a puppy in its paws, as the female.

The Eight Buddhist Emblems of Happy Augury (³³*pa chi hsiang*), Fig. 20 a to 20 h.

These are as follows:—a) The Flaming Wheel of the Law
 b) The Conch-Shell
 c) The State Umbrella
 d) The Canopy
 e) The Lotus Flower
 f) The Covered Vase
 g) The Pair of Fishes
 h) The Endless Knot.

In carpets these symbols are employed either together or singly, this being specially so in the case of the "Endless Knot" (³⁴*ch'ang*) symbolising "long duration", which is often used together with quite other symbols. (Compare central field in Fig. 52, and border of Fig. 54).

With the foregoing we have given the commonest symbols of a mystic or religious nature to be found in carpets. It should, however, be borne in mind that this method of grouping refers only to their earliest origin. To-day they are more or less the common property of the entire Chinese people : they have retained their signification,

---

³² 獅子 ³³ 八吉祥 ³⁴ 長

although shorn to a great extent of their religious character. Thus, it should not be supposed that because a carpet is decorated with Taoist symbols of longevity, its owner must necessarily be a Taoist; and the same applies to other designs.

E) MISCELLANEOUS SYMBOLS.

The Chinese have a marked preference for symbols and employ them very extensively. They consist of two kinds, either of such objects as by their very nature give the sense required, as for instance, a coin to express wealth; or of sound rebuses in which the similar sound renders the sense that is to be conveyed, such as ([35] *ch'ing*), the hanging musical stone of jade for ([36] *ch'ing*) blessing. Such symbols are especially used in silk weaving. First in order are the hundred antique symbols, of which, however, for carpet designs only the emblems of the "Eight Precious Things" and the Four Fine Arts — music, chess, calligraphy and painting — need be taken into consideration.

The Eight Precious Things ([37] *pa pao*) Fig. 21 a to 21 h are :—

 a) The Pearl
 b) The Coin
 c) The Rhombus, symbol of victory and a flourishing state
 d) The Pair of Books
 e) The Painting
 f) The Musical Stone of Jade symbolising blessing.

[35] 磬 [36] 慶 [37] 八寶

g) The Pair of Rhinoceros-horn Cups

h) The Artemisia Leaf, symbol of dignity.

The Four Fine Arts, or Treasures of the Literati ([38] *ch'in-ch'i-shu-hua*) Fig. 22 a to 22 d are the Harp, the Chessboard, the Books and the Paintings, emblems of literature and science. The Literati of traditional times were as a rule closely associated with these objects; hence the origin of the symbols. (see Fig. 52).

The Character Symbols Shou and Fu. The *Shou* is depicted round ([39] *yuan-shou-tzu*), as in Fig. 23 a; and also long ([40] *ch'ang-shou-tzu*), both forms denoting longevity. These characters signifying "Good Wishes", are most extensively used on all festive occasions in the family and the business life of the people, and in either form are usually combined with the symbol *ch'ang*, (Fig. 20 h). In this combination the symbol should therefore be read "Good Luck of Endless Duration". The character *Fu*, (Fig. 23 c), dating from prehistoric times, is probably composed of the lines of the Eight Trigrams and is one of the 12 ancient ornaments embroidered on the Imperial sacrificial robes.

The Bat ([41] *pien-fu*), Fig. 24, is a symbol of happiness and is a sound rebus, for the final character for bat ([41] *fu*) has here taken on the meaning of the ([42] *fu*) signifying happiness. This emblem is often much conventionalised into peculiar forms and combined with other

---

[38] 琴棋書畫　[39] 圓壽字　[40] 長壽字

[41] 蝙蝠　[42] 福

symbols. In Fig. 25 the bat is depicted with the peach, in which combination the meaning reads "Happiness and Long Life united" ([43] *fu-shou-shuang-ch'üan*). Combined with a tuning stone (Fig. 21 f) the meaning is "Happiness and Blessing" ([44] *fu-ch'ing*). A favourite ornament is that shown in Fig. 26, five bats surrounding the character *shou* ([45] *wu fu p'êng shou*) meaning the five great blessings :— Happiness, Wealth, Peace, Virtue and Longevity.

The Symbol of Success ([46] *pi-ting-ju-i,*) Fig. 27, is represented by the sceptre (Fig. 16) a piece of uncoined silver (the Tael) and a writing brush. This symbol is also a sound rebus.

The Three Fruits ([47] *fu-shou-san-tuo*), Fig. 28, are the "Fragrant Fingers of Buddha", the Peach and the Pomegrante. The Fragrant Fingers of Buddha ([48] *Fo-shou*) is a species of citron which, instead of being spheroid at both ends like the ordinary fruit, is split up at one end into a bunch of tapering off-shoots, which, seen from the side, resemble a grasping hand. The peach has already been mentioned (see page 20). The pomegranate ([49] *shih-liu*) signifies numerous progeny. When these symbols are united, the three fruits mean "happiness, longevity and numerous male issue".

The Butterfly ([50] *hu t'ieh*) becomes a sound rebus for great age by taking the last character for ([51] *t'ieh*), length of days. Fish ([52] *yü*) by the same process is made to mean ([53] *yü*) abundance.

[43] 福壽雙全　[44] 福慶　[45] 五蝠捧壽
[46] 必定如意　[47] 福壽三多
[48] 佛手　[49] 柘榴　[50] 蝴蝶　[51] 耋　[52] 魚　[53] 餘

24

F. TREE AND FLOWER PATTERNS.

The continuous development of carpet designs owes its loveliest inspirations to the trees and flowers of China. Natural flowers are always realistically reproduced and are seldom so conventionalised as the designs in Persian carpets, so that every species of flower is recognisable at sight. Exceptions to this rule occur only when flowers are used as field designs. Out of the so-called "Hundred Flowers Design", we shall mention only the following, which being the favourites among the Chinese are most often employed :—

The Peach Blossom ([54] *t'ao-hua*), Fig. 29, is the emblem of spring and treasured as being the blossom of the fruit of life.

The Lotus Flower ([55] *hê-hua*), Fig. 17 h and 30, is the emblem of summer. It is regarded by Buddhists as the sacred flower, on which most of the heavenly deities are depicted. As one of the attributes of the Eight Genii it is also venerated. The general regard entertained for it is not only due to its beauty but also to its utility, since both its seeds and its roots are used as articles of food.

The Chrysanthemum ([56] *chü-hua*) Fig. 31 is the emblem of autumn and signifies "long duration". It is the favourite flower of the Chinese, who have found means to cultivate it in endless varieties and colours.

The Narcissus ([57] *shui-hsien-hua*), Fig. 32, is the emblem of winter. It is generally cultivated in beautiful water-filled porcelain bowls, being in full bloom about New Year's time, when it is regarded as a good omen for the coming year.

---

[54] 桃花　[55] 荷花　[56] 菊花　[57] 水仙花

The Prunus or Plum Blossom ([58] *mei-hua*) Fig. 33, is the symbol of beauty. In carpets this blossom is often reproduced alone in the form of rosettes (see Fig. 3 b).

The Orchid ([59] *lan-hua*) Fig. 34, is valued for its wonderful fragrance. Its grass-like leaves are the origin of the antique grass presentations so often seen in Chinese decorative art.

The Bamboo ([60] *chu*) Fig. 35, is the emblem of longevity and "enduring bloom", probably on account of the hardness of its wood and the enduring green of its leaves.

The Peony ([61] *mu-tan-hua* or [62] *fu-kuei-hua*) Fig. 36, is the flower of "wealth and respectability". It is usually drawn as the contrasting ornament to the lotus blossom; but also often together with the chrysanthemum, in which case it symbolises "wealth and consideration of long duration" (see Fig. 54).

Groups of Flowers and Trees in carpet designs, as in tissues and porcelains, are seldom employed at random; but generally in connection with hard and fast rules of symbolism. Some of them are:— The peach, the lotus, the chrysanthemum and the narcissus; (or sometimes the pomegranate blossom, the plum blossom, the orchid and the gardenia) for the four seasons of the year; the pine, the bamboo and the plum-tree as symbols of friendship and long life; the plum blossom, the orchid, the bamboo and the chrysanthemum as favourite flowers.

The Lotus Flower, shown in Fig. 20 e and 37 a to 37 h. The lotus and the peony predominate among flower patterns to the same

---

[58] 梅花　[59] 蘭花　[60] 竹　[61] 牡丹花　[62] 富貴花

extent as the dragon and the phoenix among the other designs. Just as the Chinese artist has allowed his imagination great latitude in the representation of fabulous creatures, so in the treatment of the lotus he has evolved a variety of forms. The reason for this is probably religious, under Buddhist influence. Since the gods are depicted as sitting or standing on lotus flowers, there is a tendency to give to the flower so honoured a supernatural value ; hence we see the leaves shaped like the head of a sceptre (see Fig. 16) ; or again, like a conventionalised cloud. The actual form of the lotus is seen only in Fig. 37 b. In Fig. 20 e and 37 c to 37 e, it is merely hinted at by the grouping together of clouds. Fig. 37 f to 37 h also show the flower in rosette forms.

Lotus Flowers and Sprays (Fig. 38 a to 38 c). The inception of these very peculiar patterns of Indian origin is to be traced to the effort to make the whole field of the carpet as uniform as possible. The first impression they give is a strange one, with the lotus flower growing on a stem nearly a yard long without any bough, leaf or twig. The explanation of this is that the idea is not to represent the lotus flower alone ; but rather the surface of a lotus pond, which contains a number of other water-plants besides. This idea is best shown in Fig. 40 which represents a lotus pond seen from above. Here, besides the lotus flower in rosette forms, we see the foliage of other plants, while the lines shown in between are intended to suggest a gentle motion of the water. A conventionalised form of the pattern of Fig. 40 is seen in Fig. 38 a. The border ornamentation of 38 c shows an attempt of the designer to make the pattern true to life, the flowers and leaves — the latter not quite open — resembling very nearly the natural form given in Fig. 30. Designs with lotus flowers and leaves as well as with peach blossoms were especially in favour during the Ming Dynasty (1368 to 1644) and were applied to porcelain as well as to fabrics. In the 17th century the Dutch introduced them in porcelains, fabrics and carpets into Europe, where they were much admired and copied. It was from such imitations as these that the Dresden "bulb" pattern and the Copenhagen "straw" pattern are said to have been evolved.

Flowers in Rosettes. A considerable departure from the natural shape of flowers and leaves in other than the lotus is to be seen in representations of flowers, when they are depicted as rosettes in central ornamentations, (compare Fig. 41, 43 and 44).

Vases of Flowers are introduced into carpet designs in as many forms as there kinds of vases and flowers. They have only a decorative value and no signification is attached to them in their use. Only when [63] *p'ing,* meaning vase, is grouped together with other symbols would it be regarded as a sound rebus for [64]*p'ing,* peace.

ILLUSTRATIONS OF CARPETS.

The following illustrations to which reference has often been made in the course of the foregoing remarks on carpet designs, will serve to show how the designs are employed.

Wool Carpets, Fig. 39 to 42. These illustrations are taken from the designs of the carpet remnants in the Shosoin Imperial Treasury

[63] 瓶   [64] 平

at Nara in Japan. They are considered to be some of the oldest extant specimens of Chinese textile art. They date from the time of the T'ang Dynasty (A. D. 618 to 907) and afford us an evidence of the height which the art of weaving had at that period already attained. All these carpets are of small dimensions and seem to have been designed for the *k'ang,* which is a kind of bed. The designs are mostly in blue on a dark yellow ground. Fig. 39 shows rosettes of lotus blossoms : Fig. 40, lotus flowers and sprays : Fig. 41 a beautiful central ornament and single flowers : and Fig. 42 two birds, clouds, crags and plants. The two birds are grouped in the centre in the form of *Yin-Yang* (see Fig. 15) the clouds in that of a sceptre (see Fig. 16). They are also called "clouds of good luck". All the motives of this last design seem to be derived from ancient tradition.

Silk Rugs Fig. 43 to 46. These also are treasured at Nara and all that has been said of the wool carpets applies also to them. Note the central ornamentations in Fig. 43 and 44. Single and cut flowers are depicted in Fig. 45 and 46.

Wool Carpet, Fig. 47, shows an old pattern. The field is decorated with symbols mostly of Taoist origin ; the pine for continuance, the stag for prosperity, the crane for longevity and the bat for happiness. The ground colour of this carpet is dark blue, and the designs are yellow in three shades. The inner border is composed of the Chinese T pattern and the outer border or edge of the diagonal swastika.

Wool Carpet, Fig. 48, from Yarkand, in Chinese Turkestan, now in the British Museum, London. In the centre are conventionalised flowers. The corners are filled in with the recurring line pattern, and the border is composed of a sea-wave band, the Chinese T pattern and the diagonal swastika design. Size: 4 feet 3 inches by 7 feet 10 inches.

Wool Carpet, Fig. 49, is the property of the Metropolitan Museum, New York. The central figure consists of dragons of the Sung Dynasty and the four corner designs of the recurring line pattern; the border is composed of the scroll pattern and the swastika band. Colour: white ground and blue design.

Wool Carpets, Fig. 50 a to 50 c. These carpets are in the Larkin collection in London. All three have the middle field covered with a uniform pattern. Fig. 50 a is composed of the swastika field pattern, enclosing bats to signify "ten thousandfold happiness". The border is composed of halved flower rosettes and the swastika border. Fig. 50 b has a central field pattern enclosed with the Chinese key pattern and the swastika border. Fig. 50 c represents flowers in rosettes and is finished off with a swastika border.

Wool Carpet, Fig. 51, woven in Shantung, has a flower design both in the field and the border, separated by a Chinese T pattern band.

Wool Carpet, Fig 52, shows on a blue ground the eight Buddhist symbols of happy augury and the emblems of the four accomplishments of art and science. The medallion in the centre represents two phoenices in the *Yin-Yang* form, enclosed by clouds, while four celestial dragons in circles are grouped in the corners. The bats symbolise happiness; and the other corner ornaments, composed of the "fragrant finger of Buddha", the sceptre and the vase, mean "happiness, long life and peace according to desire". The border is composed, firstly of the pearl-band, followed by the swastika border and finished off with an ornamentation of dragon's heads placed between sea-waves and mountains. The same design is used, in part, in the carpet reproduced in the coloured frontispiece.

Silk Rug, Fig. 53, originates from Manchuria. It was exhibited in London in 1885 and sold for £85. It has a blue ground on which are shown flowers and geometrical designs in brilliant colours.

Silk Rug, Fig. 54, exhibited in the Durant Ruel Gallery in Paris, is of a bright red colour with a field composed of peonies and chrysanthemums. The border is formed by the pearl band, the T line and an ornamentation composed of the eight symbols of happy augury.

鍾
離
權

Chung Li-chüan,

Taoist genius.

(See text page 19)

CHAPTER III
THE COLOURS OF CHINESE CARPETS.

CHAPTER III

THE COLOURS OF CHINESE CARPETS.

The art of dyeing silk and wool was known to the Chinese long before our historical era. In old illustrations of woven fabrics mention is frequently made of the richness of their colours, and it is probable that the early carpet weavers took their colours as well as their designs from the silk industry. The oldest known pieces of carpets, dating from over a thousand years ago, in the Shosoin Imperial Treasury at Nara, bear evidence of a well developed technique of colour.

Although Chinese carpets have not the variety of colour of the Persian they nevertheless possess on the whole great splendour of colours, especially wool carpets decorated with flower designs, and silk rugs. The predominating ground-colour is yellow, blue or white, or more seldom red or green.

In the actual designs, the dragon is invariably depicted in a rich shade of yellow, as is the phoenix when it is represented together with the dragon on a blue, red or green background. Conventionalised lotus blossoms and sprays are also treated in old yellow. Realistic flower designs are naturally reproduced in their own colours. The colours of other designs are left to the taste of the designer.

Vegetable colours were almost exclusivly used in dyeing. The *"Pen-tsao-kang-mu"*, a work which treats of all the Chinese plants of utility, contains the following on the chief colour plants :

YELLOW. For this the wood of the yellow-timbered sumach-tree,

Rhus succedanea (*[65] huang-lu*) is used and also the half-opened buds of the *Sophora japonica* (*[66] huai-mi*), the husks of the seeds of the gardenia, (*Gardenia florida,* *[67] chih-tzu*) and the wood of the *Cudrania triloba* (*[68] shih*), with which substance all fabrics in yellow for the earlier imperial courts were dyed.

BLUE, the ubiquitous colour in China, is obtained from the paste of the indigo plant, (*Indigofera tinctoria* *[69] lan-tien,*) cultivated in great quantities all over China.

RED, the Chinese colour of joy, is produced from the root of the madder, (*Rubia tinctoria,* *[70] chien-ts'ao*) and from the Sappan wood, (*Caesalpinia sappan,* *[71] ssu-fang-mu*).

BLACK, is extracted from gall-nuts, (*Galla sinensis,* *[72] wu-pei-tzu*) and from the acorn (*[73] hsiang-wan-tzu*).

WHITE came into question only with regard to sheep's wool which was treated with the husks of the *Gleditschia sinensis* (*[74] tsao chiao*) and was then bleached. The Chinese used these husks instead of soap, which was unknown to them.

GREEN and all other colours were compositions of the prime colours given above.

Since the use of German aniline dyes has become known in China in recent years, the carpet weavers have frequently substituted

[65] 黃櫨　[66] 槐米　[67] 梔子　[68] 柘
[69] 藍靛　[70] 茜草　[71] 蘇枋木
[72] 五倍子　[73] 橡碗子　[74] 皂角

aniline dyes for their old and more costly vegetable dyes which are difficult to produce. This is, however, a great pity, for these dyes were intended for cotton goods mostly and not suited to carpet weaving materials. Through this the quality of the carpets has deteriorated, and it is to be hoped that the weavers will either take up the vegetable dyes again, or use such aniline dyes as are specially prepared for treatment of carpet wool.

Chang Kuo
Taoist genius
(See text page 19)

CHAPTER IV
THE WEAVING OF THE CARPET.

CHAPTER IV.

THE WEAVING OF THE CARPET.

Carpet making is a link between weaving and embroidering and is carried out on weaving looms as shown in Illustration 55 of the Industrial School at Tsinanfu. These looms seem ridiculously primitive when we consider the artistic work turned out on them. The cotton warp is stretched on beams about ten feet high, the weight of which keeps it taut. Usually several weavers work at one loom. They sit before it with the balls of various colours hanging behind them on a bamboo frame. The wool yarn is fastened to the warp, knot by knot, along the entire width of the carpet, the cotton weft being drawn through the warp and forced tightly in place against the knots by an iron comb. In order to draw the weft through the warp, the latter is held apart by levers connected with it. (In Illus. 55 these levers can be seen between the balls of wool).

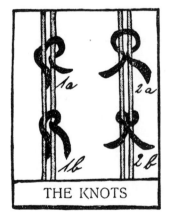

THE KNOTS

There are two kinds of knots. Both are fastened to two adjacent horizontal warp strings as shown in the illustration. Knot No. 1a or 1b is used for the centre of the carpet, while knot No. 2a or 2b is employed for finishing off the borders and ends of the carpet.

The wool knots after being firmly bound to the warp are evenly cut with an ordinary pair of scissors. Sometimes at this stage the outlines of the ornamentations are cut out, by which process the design is made to appear more plastic. This is a lengthy business, but it is justified by the improved appearance of the carpet. In weaving the design appears on the side facing the weaver. It is finer and smaller in proportion to the closeness of the warp. On a wide-meshed warp only correspondingly coarse threads and larger patterns can be worked.

CHINESE CARPETS AND RUGS

The quality of carpets in China is determined by the number of knots or threads to a foot. Wool carpets contain anything from 70, 80, 90, 100 to 110 and more threads to the foot. The 90 thread carpet is apparently the one most in demand and generally manufactured. This quality is durable and also allows the pattern to be well executed.

Silk rugs are made in the same way as wool carpets, with this difference, that the silk thread after being firmly knotted to the warp is immediately cut to the length required, because the softness of the thread, which makes it apt to tangle and fray, does not allow of the cutting being retarded. For this work a very skilful weaver is required. The fineness of the silk thread also demands a very much finer-meshed warp than the coarser wool yarn. The silk rug contains 100 to 200 knots to the foot.

The fringes found at the two ends of a carpet are the ends of the warp on which the article is woven.

何仙姑

Ho Hsien-ku
Taoist genius
(See text page 19).

APPENDIX

APPENDIX

PLATES

PLATE I

Fig. 1. The pearl-border

a   b

Fig. 2 a & b
a. "T" pattern, b. Key pattern

a   c

b

Fig. 3 a to c
Recurring-line patterns

Fig. 4
The Dice pattern.

Fig. 5
The Circle pattern

PLATE II

Fig. 6 a to 6 g
The Swastika, symbol of luck.

a
The Swastika

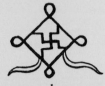

b
The Swastika in a square

c   Swastika border design

d   Swastika border design

e   Diagonal Swastika border.

f
Swastika field pattern

g
Diagonal Swastika field
pattern

PLATE III

Fig. 7
The Dragon of Heaven

a   b   c   d

e

Fig. 8 a to 8 e. The Thunder-line.

a. Hieroglyphic form for thunder.
b. Later development of a.
c. & d. Decorative compositions of b.
e. The thunder-line, composed of c.
   There is also one composed of d.

PLATE IV

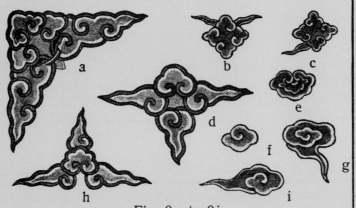

Fig. 9 a to 9 i.
The Cloud design.

Fig. 10
Cloud border.

Fig. 11
Still water.

Fig. 12
Sea waves. The little clouds over the angles
represent the sea spray.

PLATE V

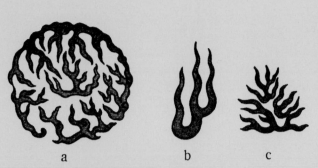

a   b   c

Fig. 13 a to c
Lightning and Fire design

a   b   c

Fig. 14 a to c. Mountains and Crags

Fig. 15

In the centre the dual Yin-Yang, the principles of being, surrounded by the eight Trigrams of divination.

Fig. 16

The sceptre of the supreme heavenly deity.

PLATE VI

YELLOW CARPET.

CARPET OF THE IMPERIAL PALACE IN PEKING,

used for the decoration of altars during the annual sacrifices; Imperial yellow ground with designs entirely in blue of several tones; the design is a Buddhistic one of Indian origin with Lotus flowers and sprays. Adjoining the centre field is the Pearl Border, followed by a border with Lotus and sprays. The main border is Swastika linked in a continuous pattern and is called by the Chinese "Wan tzu pu tao tou" or endless luck.
The size of the carpet is 5' x 8½'.

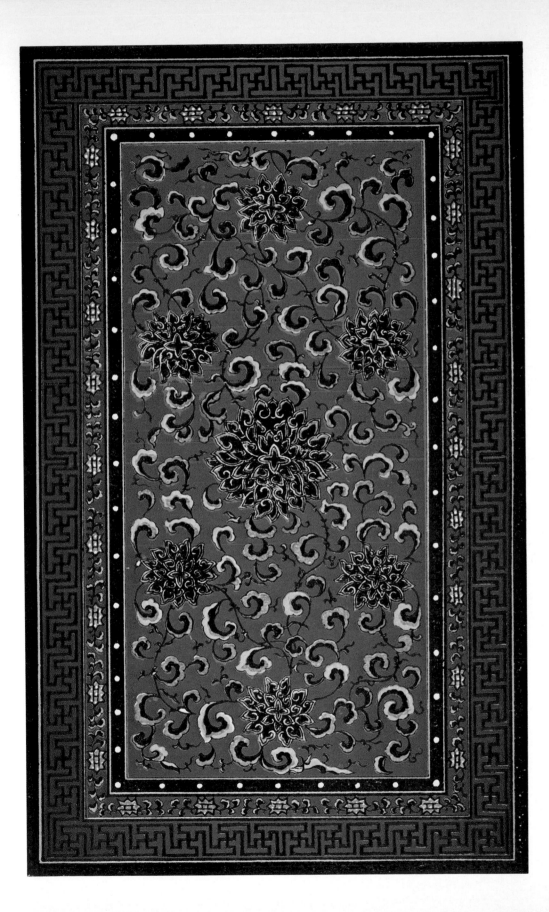

PLATE VII

Fig. 17 a to 17 h
The Attributes of the eight Taoistic Genii.

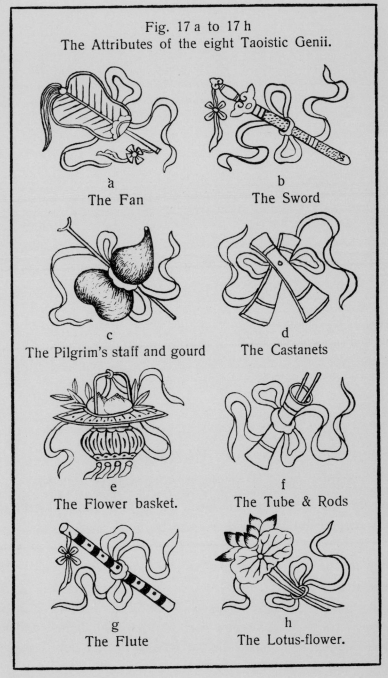

a
The Fan

b
The Sword

c
The Pilgrim's staff and gourd

d
The Castanets

e
The Flower basket.

f
The Tube & Rods

g
The Flute

h
The Lotus-flower.

PLATE VIII

RED CARPET.

CARPET OF THE IMPERIAL PALACE IN PEKING,

used for the decoration of altars during the annual sacrifices; Wine red ground filled with Incense Burners, Bowls, Vases, and floral designs. The Incense Burners bowls and vases are of all kinds called by the Chinese "Po Ku" or the "Hundred Curios". The vases in the corners are filled with lotus and peonies. In the bowls are the "Fragrant Fingers of Buddha" and the "Sacred Fungus". Next to the centre field are the Pearl border and the Lotus border. The main border consists of alternate dragons and pearls. The size of the carpet is 5' x 8½'.

PLATE IX

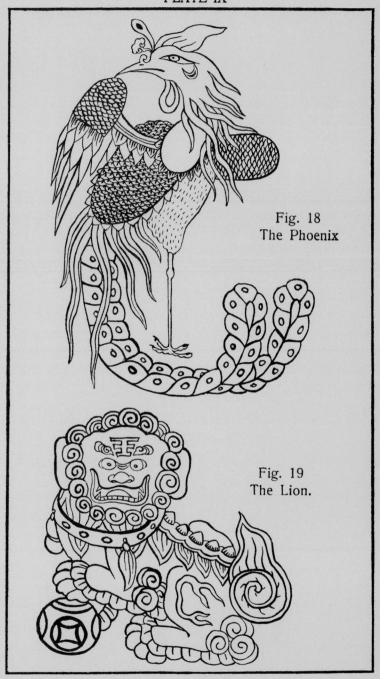

Fig. 18
The Phoenix

Fig. 19
The Lion.

PLATE X

Fig. 20 a to 20 h

The Eight Buddhist Emblems of Happy Augury.

a

The Wheel of the Law

b

The Conch-shell

c

The State Umbrella

d

The Canopy

e

The Lotus Flower

f

The Covered Vase

g

The Pair of Fishes

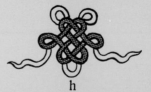

h

The Endless Knot.

PLATE XI

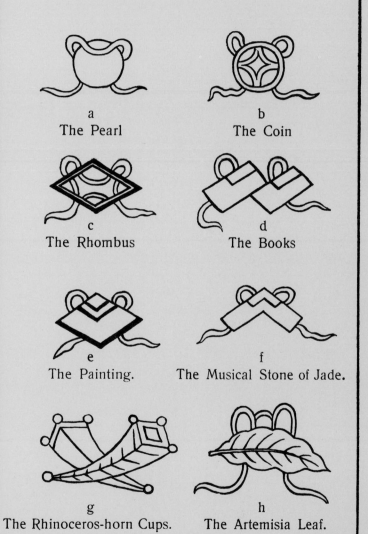

Fig. 21 a to 21 h
The Eight Precious Things.

a
The Pearl

b
The Coin

c
The Rhombus

d
The Books

e
The Painting.

f
The Musical Stone of Jade.

g
The Rhinoceros-horn Cups.

h
The Artemisia Leaf.

PLATE XII

Fig. 22 a to 22 d
The four symbols of literature and science.

a

The Harp

b

The Chessboard

c

The Books

d

The Paintings

a   b   c

Fig. 23 a to 23 c Character sign symbols.

a. The round *Shou,*
b. The long *Shou,* meaning "long life",
c. The *Fu,* meaning "happiness".

PLATE XIII

Fig. 24
The bat.

Fig. 25
Bat and peach.

Fig. 26
Five bats, surrounding the character *Shou*.

Fig. 27
Sceptre, writing brush &
uncoined silver, symbol
of success.

Fig. 28
The Three Fruits.

PLATE XIV

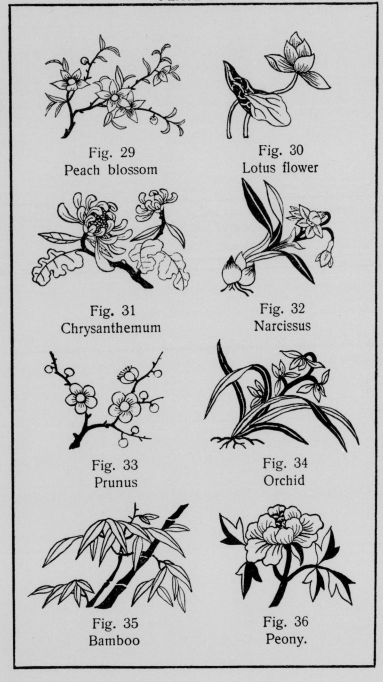

Fig. 29
Peach blossom

Fig. 30
Lotus flower

Fig. 31
Chrysanthemum

Fig. 32
Narcissus

Fig. 33
Prunus

Fig. 34
Orchid

Fig. 35
Bamboo

Fig. 36
Peony.

PLATE XV

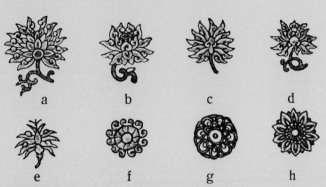

Fig. 37 a to 37 h.   Conventionalised lotus flowers.

Fig. 38 a to 38 c.
Lotus flowers and sprays.

PLATE XVI

Wool carpets dating from 8th century
in Imperial Treasury at Nara, Japan.

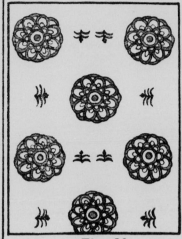

Fig. 39
Lotus flowers

Fig. 40
Lotus and sprays.

Fig. 41
Flower rosette.

Fig. 42
Birds, clouds, rocks &
plants.

(O. Münsterberg, Chinesische Kunstgeschichte, Band II.)

PLATE XVII

Silk rugs dating from the 8th century
in Imperial Treasury at Nara, Japan.

Fig. 44

Fig. 43

Flower rosette.

Flower rosette,
flower and rock border.

Fig. 45

Fig. 46

Flower pattern.

Flower pattern.

(O. Münsterberg, Chinesische Kunstgeschichte, Band II.)

PLATE XVIII

FIG. 47
WOOL CARPET.

PLATE XIX

FIG. 48
WOOL CARPET FROM YARKAND.

PLATE XX

FIG. 49

WOOL CARPET,
IN THE METROPOLITAN MUSEUM, NEW-YORK

(O. Münsterberg, Chinesische Kunstgeschichte, Band II.)

PLATE XXI

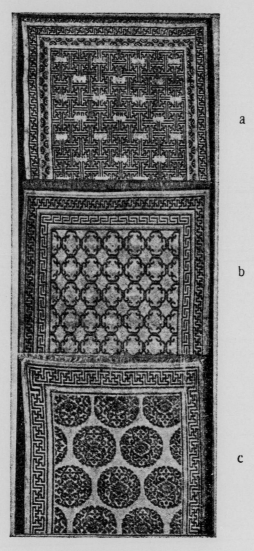

a

b

c

FIG. 50 a to 50 c
WOOL CARPETS,
LARKIN COLLECTION LONDON

(O. Münsterberg, Chinesische Kunstgeschichte, Band II.)

PLATE XXII

FIG. 51

WOOL CARPET,
WOVEN IN THE PROVINCE OF SHANTUNG.

O. Münsterberg, Chinesische Kunstgeschichte, Band II.)

PLATE XXIII

FIG. 52

WOOL CARPET.

PLATE XXIV

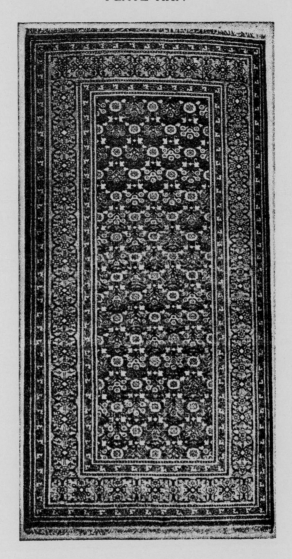

FIG. 53

SILK RUG, FROM MANCHURIA,

EXHIBITED IN LONDON 1885.

(O. Münsterberg, Chinesische Kunstgeschichte, Band II.)

PLATE XXV

FIG. 54

SILK RUG.

PLATE XXVI.

FIG. 55

CARPET LOOM

IN THE INDUSTRIAL SCHOOL AT TSINANFU, SHANTUNG.

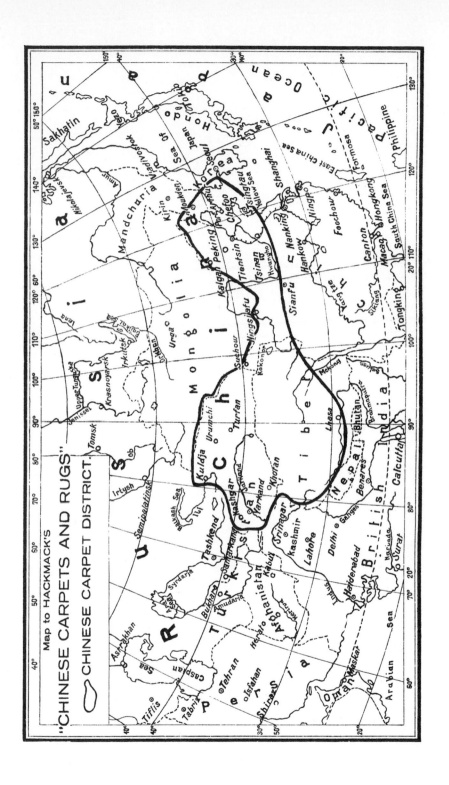

Map to HACKMACK'S
"CHINESE CARPETS AND RUGS"
CHINESE CARPET DISTRICT.